LEADING WITH
PURPOSE

*10 Steps to Cultivate
Authentic Leadership*

BY TODD M. SIMMONS

LEADING WITH PURPOSE

10 Steps to Cultivate Authentic Leadership

BY TODD M. SIMMONS

ISBN: 979-88715-04338

LEADING WITH
PURPOSE

10 Steps to Cultivate
Authentic Leadership

BY TODD M. SIMMONS

FOR YOU...

INTRODUCTION

The book "Leading with Purpose: 10 Steps to Cultivate Authentic Leadership" sets the stage for a transformative journey towards becoming an authentic leader. Recognizing the need for purpose-driven leadership in today's complex and rapidly changing world, the book provides a comprehensive roadmap to help individuals develop their leadership skills while staying true to their values and principles.

The book begins by highlighting the crucial role of authentic leadership in inspiring and motivating teams, fostering trust, and driving organizational success. It emphasizes the importance of aligning personal values with leadership practices to create a meaningful and purposeful impact on both individuals and organizations.

Furthermore, "Leading with Purpose" introduces the ten-step framework that will guide readers through their leadership development journey. Each step is carefully crafted to address key aspects of authentic leadership, including self-awareness, empathy, integrity, and vision. By following these steps, readers will gain a deep understanding of their own leadership style and how it can be refined to create a positive and lasting impact on their teams and organizations.

Moreover, the book highlights the significance of personal growth and self-reflection in the pursuit of authentic leadership. By embracing vulnerability and continuously learning from experiences, individuals can unlock their true potential as leaders and inspire others to do the same.

"Leading with Purpose" establishes a clear and concise roadmap, providing a compelling rationale for why authentic leadership is essential in today's complex business landscape. By laying the foundation for the ten-step framework, the book sets the reader up for a transformative journey towards becoming a purpose-driven and authentic leader.

To keep you up-to-date with where you should go on this project a calendar is provided.

Day	Monday	Tuesday	Wednesday	Thursday	Friday	Saturday	Sunday
Instructions	Read steps 1-5 and complete the journal entries with them	Read steps 6-10 and do the journal entries with them	Read the leadership style notes and do the journal questions	Do the qualitative approach questions	Do the quantitative approach, including the self-assessment	Do the examples section	Start the exercises (spread out as needed for your team)
Completed? (Did you do that work that day?)							
What did you learn? What can you teach to others?							
What do you need to come back to later?							

THE WHY

Authentic leadership, a concept that has gained prominence in recent years, centers around the congruence between a leader's actions and their values. It emphasizes the importance of leaders being true to themselves, fostering transparent communication, and building genuine relationships. Research on authentic leadership has illuminated its positive impact on individuals, teams, and organizations.

Dimensions of Authentic Leadership:

Authentic leadership encompasses several dimensions that contribute to its holistic framework. These dimensions include consistency between words and actions, transparent communication, self-awareness, empathy, values-driven decision-making, and the development of genuine relationships. Studies have shown that these dimensions interplay to create a leadership approach that is both effective and genuine.

Positive Impact on Individuals and Teams:

Research underscores that authentic leadership has a positive impact on individuals' well-being, job satisfaction, and engagement. Leaders who exhibit authenticity are perceived as trustworthy, approachable, and inspirational, leading to improved team cohesion and productivity. Authentic leaders' ability to foster open communication and demonstrate empathy creates a work environment where employees feel valued, supported, and motivated to contribute their best. It also leads to other people being more authentic.

Organizational Outcomes:

Organizations benefit from authentic leadership as well. Teams led by authentic leaders tend to experience lower turnover rates, reduced absenteeism, and higher levels of innovation. This leadership style promotes a culture of trust, collaboration, and shared purpose, aligning team members' efforts with the organization's goals. The effects on the team are multiplied. Authentic leaders also play a critical role in managing change and navigating complex challenges, enhancing an organization's adaptability and resilience.

Challenges and Implications:

While authentic leadership offers numerous advantages, its practice is not without challenges. Striking a balance between transparency and the need for confidentiality takes practice, and addressing potential perceptions of vulnerability while adapting authentic leadership across diverse cultural contexts are areas that require careful consideration. Furthermore, authentic leadership should not be used as an excuse for rigid or unchecked behaviors, as it requires self-awareness and continuous reflection.

Leadership Development and Training:

Research has highlighted the significance of leadership development programs that emphasize authentic leadership. These programs help leaders enhance their self-awareness, communication skills, emotional intelligence, and ethical decision-making. The integration of authentic leadership principles into training curriculum equips leaders to navigate complex organizational landscapes and effectively engage with their teams. This book is a start to training or enhancing these critical leadership skills.

Future Directions:

As the landscape of leadership continues to evolve, research on authentic leadership remains an ongoing endeavor. Scholars are exploring topics such as the role of authentic leadership in fostering diversity and inclusion, its impact in remote work environments, and its implications for various industries and sectors. Furthermore, research is addressing the potential link between authentic leadership and long-term organizational sustainability.

STEP 1:

DISCOVER YOUR PURPOSE

"Purpose driven leaders are driven by a passion to change the world. But purpose driven leaders understand that in order to change others they must first lead themselves."

MCDOWELL

Effective leadership is crucial for success in any organization. However, true leadership goes beyond simply holding a position of authority; it requires authenticity, a deep understanding of oneself, and a clear sense of purpose. Authentic leadership begins with discovering and embracing your values, passions, and what truly drives you. This process of self-reflection and introspection is essential for guiding your decisions and actions as a leader.

To embark on the journey of authentic leadership, one must first take the time to reflect on their values. Values are the principles and beliefs that guide our behavior and shape our character. They define what is important to us and what we stand for. Identifying your core values is crucial as they serve as the foundation of your leadership style and influence the way you interact with others. When your actions align with your values, you will exude authenticity, gaining the trust and respect of your team.

Moreover, understanding your passions is equally important in discovering your purpose as a leader. Passion is the fuel that ignites your motivation and drives you towards achieving your goals. It is the deep-rooted enthusiasm for a particular cause or activity. By recognizing your passions, you can channel your energy and focus towards areas that truly matter to you. This alignment between your passions and your leadership role will not only bring you fulfillment but will also inspire and motivate those around you.

Discovering your purpose goes hand in hand with understanding your values and passions. Purpose is the reason why you do what you do. It is the impact you want to make in your organization and the world. When you have clarity on your purpose, you become a visionary leader who inspires others to join you on your mission. Your purpose serves as a compass, guiding your decisions and actions. It gives you direction and helps you prioritize what is truly important. Without a clear purpose, leaders can easily get lost in the noise and distractions of daily tasks, losing sight of their true impact.

Authentic leadership begins with understanding your values, passions, and what truly drives you. By taking the time to reflect on your purpose and the impact you want to make, you gain clarity and direction as a leader. This clarity guides your decisions and actions, allowing you to lead authentically and inspire others.

Purpose is something innate in people, and yet you may not know you have it. It is similar to the phrase "if it was important enough, you would make time for it". Obviously, this is an oversimplification. However, if you look at what you spend time doing, it could be related to your purpose.

You also can use some of the journal questions below to think through this more completely.

DISCUSSION QUESTIONS

1. How do you define purposeful leadership and why is it important in today's business environment?

2. What steps have you taken personally to develop your own purpose?

....

....

....

....

....

....

....

....

....

....

....

....

....

....

....

....

3. Fill out this chart as you work through the journaling and feedback.

STRENGTHS	WEAKNESSES	BLIND SPOTS

REFLECTION

STEP 2:

LEAD WITH INTEGRITY

"Authentic leadership is built on a foundation of trust, transparency, and genuine care for those you lead."

SIMON SINEK

Effective leadership is more important than ever. It is not enough for leaders to simply give commands and make decisions; they must also inspire and motivate their team to achieve their goals. One of the key qualities that sets successful leaders apart is their integrity. Authentic leaders understand the importance of aligning their words with their actions and consistently demonstrate ethical behavior. By doing so, they build trust with their team and create an environment that fosters collaboration and success.

Consistency in behavior is a crucial aspect of leadership. Authentic leaders understand that their actions speak louder than words. They strive to be consistent in their behavior, regardless of the circumstances. This consistency creates a sense of stability and predictability that allows their team to trust and follow them. When leaders are inconsistent or flip-flop on their decisions, it creates confusion and erodes trust. Authentic leaders recognize the impact their behavior has on their team and make a conscious effort to be consistent in their actions.

Accountability is another important aspect of leading with integrity. Authentic leaders hold themselves accountable for their actions and decisions. They do not shy away from taking responsibility for their mistakes or failures. By doing so, they set an example for their team and create a culture of accountability. When leaders hold themselves accountable, it encourages their team members to do the same. This fosters a sense of ownership and responsibility within the team, leading to increased productivity and success.

Leading with integrity is a powerful way to build trust with your team. Authentic leaders understand that actions speak louder than words. They strive to be role models for their team by demonstrating the behavior and values they expect from others. By consistently acting in an ethical and transparent manner, leaders earn the trust and respect of their team. When team members see their leader practicing what they preach, it creates a sense of credibility and authenticity that is essential for effective leadership. They are dependable.

Building trust with your team is crucial for creating a positive and productive work environment. Authentic leaders understand that trust is earned and not given. They proactively work on building trust by demonstrating honesty, transparency, and ethical behavior. They communicate openly and honestly with their team, keeping them informed about important decisions and changes. They treat their team members with respect and fairness, valuing their opinions and contributions. By leading with integrity, leaders create an environment where trust flourishes. This leads to increased collaboration, engagement, and ultimately, success.

Leading with integrity is a fundamental aspect of effective leadership. Authentic leaders align their words with their actions, consistently demonstrate ethical behavior, hold themselves accountable, and lead by example. By doing so, they build trust with their team and create an environment that fosters collaboration and success. In today's complex and rapidly changing world, the importance of integrity in leadership cannot be overstated. Aspiring leaders should strive to lead with integrity, as it is not only the right thing to do, but also the key to long-term success.

DISCUSSION QUESTIONS

1. How do you foster a culture of integrity and transparency within your organization?

2. Can you share an example of a situation where you had to make a difficult decision while staying true to your integrity?

3. Fill out this chart as you work through the journaling
and feedback.

STRENGTHS	WEAKNESSES	BLIND SPOTS

REFLECTION

STEP 3:

PRACTICE SELF-AWARENESS

"To be an authentic leader, one must have the humility to admit mistakes and the courage to learn from them."

ANGELA AHRENDTS

In the pursuit of personal growth and authentic leadership, one must prioritize self-awareness. This crucial skill enables individuals to understand their strengths, weaknesses, and blind spots, fostering growth and development in both professional and personal realms. Living this out will require personal work to match professional changes. By seeking feedback from others and being open to constructive criticism, individuals can gain valuable insights into their behaviors and actions, allowing for continuous self-improvement and enhanced relationships.

Understanding one's strengths is essential for personal growth and success. When individuals possess a deep understanding of their unique abilities, they can leverage these strengths to excel in their chosen endeavors. By recognizing their strengths, individuals can focus their energy on areas where they naturally thrive, resulting in increased productivity and satisfaction. Moreover, self-awareness empowers individuals to strategically align their strengths with their goals, enabling them to make informed decisions and pursue meaningful opportunities that align with their capabilities. For some people, these are the easiest truths to find, and for others, they are the hardest. You have strengths. Ask for help if you are still stuck, and that is the rule for the next two parts as well.

Equally important is the recognition of one's weaknesses. Self-awareness allows individuals to identify areas in which they may be lacking or require development. Rather than ignoring or denying these weaknesses, self-aware individuals embrace them as opportunities for growth. By acknowledging their limitations, individuals can seek out learning opportunities, training, or mentorship to improve their skills. Growth is the goal. This dedication to self-improvement not only enhances their abilities but also demonstrates a commitment to personal growth, garnering respect and admiration from peers and subordinates.

However, self-awareness extends beyond recognizing strengths and weaknesses; it also involves identifying blind spots. Blind spots refer to aspects of ourselves that we are unaware of or fail to perceive accurately. These blind spots can hinder personal growth and authentic leadership if left unaddressed. Seeking feedback from others is instrumental in uncovering these blind spots. By actively soliciting input and perspectives from colleagues, mentors, or even friends and family, individuals gain valuable insights into their behaviors, attitudes, and actions that may not align with their intended impact. This feedback provides an opportunity for self-reflection and enables individuals to address any misalignments between their intentions and the perceptions of others.

Being open to constructive criticism is crucial in the process of self-awareness. While receiving feedback can be challenging, it is essential to approach it with an open mind and a willingness to learn and grow. Constructive criticism allows individuals to see their blind spots from an objective standpoint, providing an opportunity for self-correction and improvement. By embracing feedback and viewing it as an opportunity for growth rather than a personal attack, individuals can foster a culture of continuous learning and development.

Starting these conversations that are kind, expressing what you want to know and how you want it shared to you, can make it less overwhelming.

Self-awareness also necessitates continuous reflection on one's actions and their impact on others. This introspection enables individuals to evaluate the consequences of their behavior, both positive and negative, and make necessary adjustments. By reflecting on their interactions, decisions, and communication styles, individuals can identify areas for improvement and refine their approach to achieve better outcomes. This reflective practice not only enhances personal growth but also contributes to the development of authentic leadership.

Self-awareness is a key driver of personal growth and authentic leadership. By understanding our strengths, weaknesses, and blind spots, we can leverage our abilities, address areas for improvement, and seek feedback to enhance our self-awareness. Continuous reflection on our actions and their impact on others further contributes to personal growth and the development of authentic leadership. As we strive for excellence in our personal and professional lives, let us prioritize self-awareness as a foundational skill for growth and success.

DISCUSSION QUESTIONS

1. What are some of your strengths and weaknesses and how can you build on them?

_____

_____

_____

_____

_____

_____

_____

_____

_____

_____

_____

_____

_____

_____

_____

2. How do you actively seek feedback from your team members and stakeholders to recognize and improve your blind spots?

3. Fill out this chart as you work through the journaling and feedback.

STRENGTHS	WEAKNESSES	BLIND SPOTS

REFLECTION

STEP 4:

DEVELOP EMOTIONAL INTELLIGENCE

"Authentic leadership is not about seeking personal glory, but about creating a legacy of positive change that outlasts your tenure."

MARY BARRA

Developing emotional intelligence is crucial for effective leadership. Authentic leaders who possess emotional intelligence are better able to understand and connect with their team members' experiences and emotions. By actively listening, showing empathy, and fostering a supportive work environment, leaders can cultivate their emotional intelligence and create a positive impact on their teams.

Active listening is a crucial skill for developing emotional intelligence. Leaders who actively listen demonstrate their commitment to understanding their team members' thoughts and feelings. Active listening involves not only hearing what is being said but also paying attention to non-verbal cues and emotions. By truly listening, leaders can develop a deeper understanding of their team members' needs and concerns, which helps build trust and rapport within the team. Showing you are actively listening also helps. This can be done by showing attention to the person, especially asking clarifying questions. Active listening also makes sure that you have all the necessary information to make informed decisions.

Moreover, emotional intelligence goes beyond just understanding and listening; it also involves expressing compassion and support. Authentic leaders who demonstrate this can create a safe space for their team members to express their emotions and concerns. By acknowledging and validating these emotions, leaders can help their team members feel understood and valued. This support fosters a positive work environment where team members feel comfortable sharing their thoughts and ideas, ultimately leading to increased engagement and productivity.

In addition to active listening, creating a supportive work environment is essential for developing emotional intelligence. A supportive work environment encourages open communication, collaboration, and personal growth. Leaders who actively promote a culture of support and respect can help their team members feel valued and motivated. This environment allows team members to feel comfortable expressing their emotions and seeking guidance when needed. By creating a safe space for emotional expression, leaders can foster stronger relationships and build a high-performing team. Safe spaces have become a buzzword, but it is not about not offending people as much as it is about encouraging honesty and decision making. This can be done by being honest yourself, highlighting people who make creative innovations, and offering open times for people to talk— even if it is to complain about their day.

Developing emotional intelligence is crucial for authentic leaders. Active listening and a supportive work environment are key components of emotional intelligence. By cultivating these skills, leaders can better understand and connect with their team members, leading to improved performance and engagement. As leaders, it is important to prioritize emotional intelligence and continuously strive to create a positive and empathetic work environment.

DISCUSSION QUESTIONS

1. Can you share an example of a time when you had to make a decision that required emotional intelligence, and how did you navigate that situation?

2. Who can you actively listen to today, and what information can you deliver with tact?

3. Fill out this chart as you work through the journaling and feedback.

STRENGTHS	WEAKNESSES	BLIND SPOTS

REFLECTION

STEP 5:

BUILD MEANINGFUL RELATIONSHIPS

"Authentic leaders inspire and empower others by leading with empathy, compassion, and a genuine desire to make a positive impact."

MELINDA GATES

Authentic leadership is built on strong relationships. Take the time to connect with your team members on a personal level. Show genuine interest in their well-being and professional growth. Foster an inclusive and collaborative culture where everyone feels valued and heard.

The nature of leadership has evolved significantly. Gone are the days when leaders were merely expected to provide guidance and make decisions. The modern leader is someone who understands the importance of building meaningful relationships with their team members.

Authentic leadership is built on strong relationships. It goes beyond the superficial interactions and requires leaders to invest time and effort in connecting with their team members on a personal level. This means taking the time to get to know them as individuals, understanding their strengths, weaknesses, blind spots, and aspirations. It means showing genuine interest in their well-being and professional growth.

When leaders take the time to build meaningful relationships, a sense of trust and loyalty is established. Team members feel valued and appreciated, knowing that their leader genuinely cares about their success. This, in turn, leads to increased motivation, engagement, and productivity.

Fostering an inclusive and collaborative culture is another essential aspect of building meaningful relationships. Inclusion means creating an environment where everyone feels welcome and valued, regardless of their background or characteristics. It requires leaders to actively listen to different perspectives, encourage diverse voices, and promote a sense of belonging.

Collaboration is also crucial in building strong relationships. When leaders foster a culture of collaboration, team members feel empowered to contribute their ideas and opinions. They are more likely to feel like part of a team, working towards a common goal. This not only enhances the quality of work produced but also creates a sense of camaraderie and shared purpose.

Building meaningful relationships also involves effective communication. Leaders must be open and transparent in their communication, ensuring that team members are well-informed and aware of the organization's goals and objectives. Regular communication channels, such as team meetings, one-on-one conversations, and feedback sessions, can help facilitate this process.

However, building meaningful relationships is not a one-time effort. It requires continuous investment and nurturing. Leaders must consistently make an effort to connect with their team members, even when faced with time constraints or busy schedules. Small gestures, like checking in on their well-being or recognizing their achievements, can go a long way in strengthening relationships.

Authentic leadership is built on strong relationships. Leaders who take the time to connect with their team members on a personal level, show genuine interest in their well-being, and foster an inclusive and collaborative culture, are more likely to succeed in today's dynamic business environment. By building meaningful relationships, leaders can create a sense of trust, loyalty, and engagement, ultimately driving organizational success.

It may seem against the spirit of it to put this on the calendar, but doing whatever you can to make sure you do this regularly can create a pattern. It will become a natural habit over time.

DISCUSSION QUESTIONS

1. What relationships are already strong and where can you build on other relationships?

2. How do you integrate your coworkers' lives into your authentic leadership practices?

3. Fill out this chart as you work through the journaling and feedback.

STRENGTHS	WEAKNESSES	BLIND SPOTS

REFLECTION

STEP 6:

COMMUNICATE EFFECTIVELY

"The art of communication is the language of leadership."

JAMES HUMES

In the realm of leadership, communication plays a pivotal role in establishing authenticity and fostering trust within a team or organization. Clear and transparent communication serves as the foundation for effective leadership, enabling leaders to connect with their team members, understand their concerns, and inspire them to achieve common goals. Authentic leaders understand the importance of open, honest, and timely communication, as well as the significance of active listening and creating a safe space for honest conversations.

To communicate effectively, it is crucial for leaders to be open and transparent in their communication. Authentic leaders understand that withholding information or manipulating facts can erode trust and create a sense of uncertainty among team members. By sharing information openly and honestly, leaders demonstrate their commitment to transparency and establish an environment of trust and integrity. When team members feel that their leaders are being forthright and honest, they are more likely to reciprocate this behavior and engage in open and honest communication themselves.

Furthermore, timely communication is essential in authentic leadership. Delayed or insufficient communication can lead to misunderstandings, confusion, and even conflict within a team. Leaders must be proactive in sharing information, updates, and decisions to ensure that their team members are well-informed and able to carry out their responsibilities effectively. By keeping the lines of communication open and providing timely updates, leaders demonstrate their respect for their team members' time and efforts, fostering a sense of trust and commitment.

Encouraging open dialogue and creating a safe space for honest conversations is a hallmark of authentic leadership. Leaders should create an environment where team members feel comfortable speaking up, sharing their opinions, and challenging the status quo.

This cultivates a culture of innovation, collaboration, and continuous improvement. When leaders actively encourage open dialogue and value diverse perspectives, they foster creativity, problem-solving, and a sense of ownership among team members.

Effective communication is vital for authentic leadership. Leaders must strive to be open, honest, and timely in their communication, ensuring transparency and trust within the team or organization. Active listening and encouraging open dialogue further enhance the authenticity of leaders, allowing them to connect with their team members, understand their concerns, and inspire them to reach their full potential. By prioritizing effective communication, leaders can create an environment that encourages collaboration, innovation, and growth, leading to the achievement of common goals.

DISCUSSION QUESTIONS

1. How do you communicate your vision and goals to your team members in a way that inspires and motivates them?

2. How do you promote a sense of ownership and accountability among your team members while still maintaining your authentic leadership style?

3. Fill out this chart as you work through the journaling and feedback.

STRENGTHS	WEAKNESSES	BLIND SPOTS

REFLECTION

STEP 7:

ENCOURAGE INNOVATION AND CREATIVITY

"If an organization values innovation, you can assume it's safe to speak up with new ideas, leaders will listen, and your voice matters."

ADAM GRANT

Innovation and creativity have become crucial for organizations to stay competitive and thrive. Authentic leaders understand the importance of empowering their teams to think outside the box, take risks, and bring forth fresh ideas. They encourage innovation through various means, such as providing opportunities for brainstorming, experimentation, and learning from failure. Furthermore, these leaders acknowledge and celebrate the innovative ideas and contributions of their team members, creating a culture that values and rewards creativity.

One of the keyways authentic leaders encourage innovation is by providing opportunities for brainstorming. They understand that great ideas can come from anyone, regardless of their position or experience level. These leaders create a space where team members feel comfortable sharing their thoughts and suggestions. They actively seek input from their team by organizing brainstorming sessions where everyone can contribute their ideas and perspectives. By encouraging open dialogue and diverse thinking, authentic leaders stimulate creativity and generate innovative solutions to challenges faced by the organization.

Experimentation is another crucial aspect of fostering innovation. Authentic leaders understand that not all ideas will succeed, but they believe in the value of trying and learning from failure. They encourage their teams to experiment with new approaches, technologies, and processes. By providing the necessary resources and support, these leaders enable their team members to explore and test their ideas. They understand that failure is not a setback but rather an opportunity for growth and improvement. Through experimentation, teams can identify what works and what doesn't, leading to the development of innovative and effective solutions.

Learning from failure is an integral part of the innovation process. Authentic leaders create an environment where failure is not stigmatized but rather seen as a stepping-stone towards success. They encourage their teams to reflect on their failures, analyze what went wrong, and extract valuable lessons from the experience. By promoting a growth mindset, these leaders inspire their team members to persist in the face of adversity and view setbacks as learning opportunities. This mindset fosters resilience and encourages individuals to continue exploring new ideas and pushing boundaries.

Celebrating and recognizing innovative ideas and contributions is another important aspect of encouraging innovation. Authentic leaders understand the significance of acknowledging and appreciating the efforts of their team members. They create a culture where innovative ideas are celebrated and rewarded. They publicly recognize individuals who have made significant contributions to the organization's success through their creativity and out-of-the-box thinking. By doing so, these leaders not only motivate the individual being recognized but also inspire others to think innovatively and strive for excellence.

Authentic leaders will continue to play a vital role in encouraging innovation and creativity within their teams. By providing opportunities for brainstorming, experimentation, and learning from failure, they create an environment that encourages psychological safety. Moreover, by celebrating and recognizing innovative ideas and contributions, these leaders cultivate a culture that values and rewards creativity. Organizations need authentic leaders who can empower their teams to think creatively and take risks, ultimately driving innovation and ensuring long-term success.

DISCUSSION QUESTIONS

1. What steps do you take to continuously be innovative and creative?

2. How can you encourage your team members to be innovative and creative?

3. Fill out this chart as you work through the journaling and feedback.

STRENGTHS	WEAKNESSES	BLIND SPOTS

REFLECTION

STEP 8:

FOSTER A GROWTH MINDSET

"Without continual growth and progress, such words as improvement, achievement and success have no meaning."

BENJAMIN FRANKLIN

It is essential to foster a growth mindset within your team and yourself. A growth mindset is the belief that abilities and intelligence can be developed through dedication, effort, and learning. By embracing challenges, learning from setbacks, and continuously seeking opportunities for growth and development, you and your team can unlock new levels of success and achieve your full potential.

One of the first steps in cultivating a growth mindset is to embrace challenges. Instead of shying away from difficult tasks, view them as opportunities for growth and development. Challenges provide a chance to stretch your abilities, learn new skills, and expand your knowledge. By taking on challenges head-on, you demonstrate a willingness to learn and grow, inspiring your team members to do the same.

Learning from setbacks is another crucial aspect of fostering a growth mindset. Setbacks and failures are inevitable in any endeavor, but it is how we respond to them that truly matters. Instead of dwelling on the negative, encourage your team to see setbacks as learning experiences. Encourage them to analyze what went wrong, identify areas for improvement, and devise strategies to overcome obstacles in the future. By reframing setbacks as opportunities for growth, you create a culture of resilience and continuous improvement.

Continuous learning is a cornerstone of a growth mindset. Encourage your team members to prioritize their professional development and provide them with the necessary resources and support. This can include offering training programs, workshops, or allocated time for self-directed learning. The examples and exercises later in this book are a good start. By investing in your team's growth, you not only enhance their skills and knowledge but also create a positive and engaged work environment.

Supporting your team members' professional development goals is essential. Take the time to understand their aspirations and help them create a plan to achieve them. Provide them with opportunities to take on new responsibilities, work on challenging projects, or collaborate with other teams. By creating a culture that values and supports individual growth, you empower your team members to reach their full potential.

Fostering a growth mindset within your team and you are crucial in today's dynamic and competitive world. By embracing challenges, learning from setbacks, and continuously seeking opportunities for growth and development, you and your team can unlock new levels of success. Encourage a culture of continuous learning and support your team members' professional development goals. By doing so, you create a positive and thriving work environment where everyone can thrive and achieve their goals.

DISCUSSION QUESTIONS

1. How do you ensure that your leadership style grows with the values and mission of the organization?

2. How do you constantly improve in your role as leader?

3. Fill out this chart as you work through the journaling and feedback.

STRENGTHS	WEAKNESSES	BLIND SPOTS

REFLECTION

STEP 9:

LEAD WITH EMPATHY

"In the realm of authentic leadership, vulnerability is not a weakness, but a strength that fosters connection and growth."

SHERYL SANDBERG

Today, leaders are often encouraged to focus on strategy, results, and profitability. While these aspects are undoubtedly crucial, authentic leaders understand that there is another equally important element to consider - empathy. This is more than developing emotional intelligence as mentioned earlier. By putting themselves in others' shoes with empathy, leaders can gain insights into their team members' perspectives, needs, and challenges. By showing compassion, understanding, and support towards team members' challenges and personal circumstances, leaders can create a culture of inclusivity, trust, and well-being, ultimately leading to increased productivity and success.

Authentic leaders recognize that their team members are not just cogs in the machine but human beings with unique emotions, aspirations, and struggles. They make a conscious effort to connect with their employees on a personal level, demonstrating genuine care and concern. By taking the time to listen actively and understandingly to their team members' concerns, leaders show that they value and respect their perspectives.

Supporting the well-being of team members goes beyond just listening; it involves actively seeking ways to alleviate their challenges. Empathetic leaders are attuned to the individual needs of their employees and provide the necessary resources and support to help them succeed. Whether it is offering flexible work arrangements, providing access to counseling services, or implementing wellness programs, authentic leaders prioritize the overall well-being of their team members. They understand that a healthy work-life balance is essential for productivity and happiness, and they encourage their employees to take time off, recharge, and pursue personal interests.

Furthermore, empathetic leaders are aware that life does not stop at the office doors. They acknowledge that their team members have personal lives and responsibilities outside of work that may impact their performance. They can demonstrate understanding and flexibility towards family emergencies, childcare needs, or personal crises. This way, leaders create an environment where employees feel valued and supported. This not only enhances employee morale but also fosters loyalty and commitment towards the organization.

Leading with empathy is not a sign of weakness, but rather a strength that authentic leaders possess. By understanding the importance of empathy in fostering a positive work environment, leaders can create a culture where employees feel valued, supported, and inspired. Compassion, understanding, and support are not just buzzwords; they are the foundation of successful organizations. So, strive to lead with empathy, creating workplaces where individuals can thrive, and success will become a natural outcome.

DISCUSSION QUESTIONS

1. Can you provide an example of a time when you had to navigate a situation where empathy and your authentic leadership style clashed with organizational expectations or norms?

2. How do you encourage diversity and inclusion within your leadership team, and how does this contribute to empathetic and authentic leadership?

3. Fill out this chart as you work through the journaling and feedback.

STRENGTHS	WEAKNESSES	BLIND SPOTS

REFLECTION

STEP 10:

LEAD WITH PURPOSE

"The mark of a truly authentic leader is their ability to inspire others to reach their full potential."

BRENÉ BROWN

Finally, authentic leaders lead with a clear purpose and vision. Once you have discovered your purpose, it is important to continuously reflect on it and reassess its relevance in your leadership journey. As individuals grow and evolve, their purpose may also evolve. Therefore, it is essential to regularly revisit your purpose and ensure that it remains aligned with your values and passions. The impact you aspire to make can also keep you on the right track. This ongoing reflection will enable you to stay true to yourself and lead authentically, even amidst challenges and uncertainties.

In addition, communicate your organization's mission and values to your team and align their work with these goals. Inspire and motivate your team by connecting their work to a higher purpose and the positive impact they can make.

Effective leadership is crucial for the success and growth of any organization. While leadership styles may vary, one aspect that remains constant is the importance of leading with purpose. Authentic leaders understand the significance of having a clear vision and purpose, and they effectively communicate this to their teams. By clearly defining the purpose and core values of the organization, leaders provide their teams with a sense of direction and a common goal to work towards. This clarity helps to create a cohesive and focused team, as everyone understands the bigger picture and the desired outcome.

When leaders communicate the mission and values of the organization, they also create a sense of alignment within the team. By aligning the work of each individual with the overall goals of the organization, leaders ensure that everyone is moving in the same direction. This alignment not only increases productivity but also enhances employee satisfaction and engagement. When employees understand how their work contributes to the larger purpose, they feel a greater sense of fulfillment and motivation.

By emphasizing the positive impact that their work can make, leaders create a sense of meaning and significance in the daily tasks of their employees. This connection to a higher purpose helps to foster a sense of passion and dedication within the team. When employees believe that their work is making a difference, they are more likely to go above and beyond to achieve excellence.

Leading with purpose is a fundamental aspect of authentic leadership. By clearly communicating the organization's mission and values, aligning the work of the team with these goals, and connecting their work to a higher purpose, leaders inspire and motivate their teams to achieve greatness. The impact of purpose-driven leadership extends beyond the organization itself, as it empowers individuals to make a positive difference in the world. As aspiring leaders, we must strive to lead with purpose and create a lasting impact on those we lead.

DISCUSSION QUESTIONS

1. How do you go from finding your purpose to leading with purpose?

2. What is this most important idea in this section of the book for your authentic leadership journey?

....

....

....

....

....

....

....

....

....

....

....

....

....

....

....

....

....

3. Fill out this chart as you work through the journaling and feedback.

STRENGTHS	WEAKNESSES	BLIND SPOTS

REFLECTION

CONCLUSION

"Leading with Purpose: 10 Steps to Cultivate Authentic Leadership" serves as a guiding light for individuals committed to not just leading, but leading with purpose. Throughout this illuminating journey, readers have been invited to embark on a transformative exploration of what it truly means to be an authentic leader – one who not only drives results but also touches the hearts and minds of those they lead.

As we close this chapter, we recognize that authentic leadership is not a destination but an ongoing voyage. The ten steps offered here are not merely checkboxes to be completed but rather a dynamic framework to be continuously cultivated and refined. They remind us that authentic leadership is a journey of growth, where embracing vulnerability, fostering empathy, and nurturing a sense of purpose become lifelong companions. We understand that leadership is a privilege and a responsibility – an opportunity to empower, inspire, and create meaningful change in the lives of those we lead and the communities they serve.

The lessons contained within these pages remind us that authentic leadership is a holistic endeavor, intertwining personal well-being with professional excellence. By fostering emotional intelligence, nurturing resilience, and embracing mindfulness, we can navigate challenges with grace and steer our teams toward success with compassion.

In the end, "Leading with Purpose" calls us to embark on a transformative journey – a journey that leads us from the surface-level trappings of leadership to the very heart of what it means to inspire, to influence, and to make a lasting impact. By integrating the ten steps into our leadership approach, we not only enhance our own lives but also ripple out positive change into the lives of those we touch.

As the final chapter comes to a close, let us remember that authentic leadership is not bound by the confines of these pages; it lives within us, waiting to be nurtured and shared. May this book continue to serve as a guiding companion for all those who aspire to lead with purpose, fostering a legacy of authenticity, impact, and meaningful connection.

To further enhance your exploration of authentic

leadership, we offer the following resources for both individual and team development. These materials aim to support your ongoing journey towards cultivating authenticity in leadership.

LEADERSHIP STYLES

Authentic leadership is influenced by diverse leadership models that prioritize traits like integrity, transparency, and authentic interactions. Explore the insights of 10 leadership models associated with authenticity. Recognizing that individuals possess varying strengths and styles, each model offers valuable lessons. Reflect on these models with accompanying questions to deepen your understanding.

Transformational Leadership:

Transformational leadership emphasizes inspiring and motivating followers through a leader's passion, vision, and charisma. Authentic leaders often exhibit transformational qualities, as they lead by example and empower their teams to achieve their full potential.

Servant Leadership:

Servant leadership centers around putting the needs of others first and serving the greater good. Authentic leaders, who genuinely care about their team members' well-being, align with the servant leadership model by encouraging their team's work-life balance and professional health.

Relational Leadership:

Relational leadership underscores the importance of building strong interpersonal relationships with team members. Authentic leaders excel in this model, as they prioritize open communication, empathy, and trust in their interactions.

Ethical Leadership:

Ethical leadership emphasizes making moral and principled decisions. Authentic leaders, with their commitment to congruence between values and actions, align closely with ethical leadership by demonstrating integrity, transparency, and ethical decision-making.

Cultural Leadership:

Cultural leadership recognizes the significance of considering cultural contexts in leadership practices. Authentic leaders embrace cultural diversity, communicate authentically across cultural boundaries, and show respect for diverse viewpoints.

Distributed Leadership:

Distributed leadership distributes decision-making authority across the team. Authentic leaders, by valuing input from their team members and encouraging open dialogue, create an environment conducive to distributed leadership practices.

Resonant Leadership:

Resonant leadership focuses on emotional intelligence and creating positive emotional experiences within the team. Authentic leaders, with their ability to connect on a genuine level, create resonant relationships that enhance team morale and motivation.

Positive Leadership:

Positive leadership emphasizes fostering a positive work environment and focusing on strengths rather than weaknesses. Authentic leaders, through their transparent communication and focus on building genuine relationships, contribute to positive leadership practices.

Collaborative Leadership:

Collaborative leadership highlights the importance of teamwork and shared decision-making. Authentic leaders naturally excel in collaboration by valuing others' perspectives, building trust, and encouraging open communication.

Inclusive Leadership:

Inclusive leadership promotes diversity, equity, and inclusion. Authentic leaders, with their commitment to treating all team members with respect and creating an inclusive environment, align with the principles of inclusive leadership.

These leadership models, while distinct, share common principles with authentic leadership, making them complementary and often intertwined in practice. Authentic leaders draw from these models to create a leadership approach that resonates with their values, fosters trust, and cultivates meaningful relationships within their teams.

DISCUSSION QUESTIONS

1. What leadership style do you exemplify best and why?

....

....

....

....

....

....

....

....

....

....

....

....

....

....

....

....

2. What is one leadership style that feels important, but you do not currently exemplify as well as others?

3. What leadership styles can you help other people grow in?

....

....

....

....

....

....

....

....

....

....

....

....

....

....

....

....

A COMBINATION OF QUALITATIVE AND QUANTITATIVE APPROACHES TO MEASURE AND UNDERSTAND A LEADER'S AUTHENTICITY

Leadership, a cornerstone of organizational success, has evolved beyond the traditional hierarchical model to embrace authenticity as a vital attribute. Authentic leadership, characterized by congruence between leaders' actions and values, has gained prominence due to its positive impact on team morale, employee engagement, and overall organizational performance. As organizations seek ways to assess and understand the authenticity of their leaders, a combination of qualitative and quantitative approaches emerges as a comprehensive methodology. This section delves into the nuances of employing qualitative and quantitative methods to measure and understand a leader's authenticity.

QUALITATIVE APPROACHES

Qualitative research techniques provide depth and context to the assessment of authenticity in leadership. These approaches focus on understanding the subjective experiences, emotions, and motivations that contribute to a leader's authenticity.

This part is entirely customizable based on your preferences, but these exercises are certainly worthwhile. If you encounter any challenges, seeking input from fellow leaders can provide valuable insights. Take some time to review these exercises as you initiate the process.

1. In-Depth Interviews:

In-depth interviews facilitate candid discussions between researchers and leaders, offering insights into their beliefs, values, and experiences. Open-ended questions can uncover personal narratives that illustrate moments of authenticity, challenges faced, and strategies employed to maintain congruence between actions and values. Such narratives provide rich data for understanding the multifaceted nature of authenticity.

2. Ethnographic Studies:

Ethnography involves immersing researchers in the leaders' environment, observing their interactions and behaviors in context. By studying leaders in their natural settings, ethnography captures subtle nuances of authenticity, such as nonverbal cues, communication styles, and decision-making processes. This approach allows researchers to explore how leaders demonstrate authenticity in everyday scenarios.

3. Content Analysis:

Analyzing written or verbal content, such as speeches, interviews, or internal communications, can reveal themes related to authenticity. Researchers identify keywords, phrases, and recurring messages that reflect a leader's values and principles. Content analysis provides an objective way to quantify qualitative data, bridging the gap between subjective experiences and measurable attributes.

QUANTITATIVE APPROACHES

Quantitative research methods offer structured and measurable data that enable statistical analysis of authenticity-related factors. These methods are valuable for assessing trends, correlations, and patterns across a larger sample of leaders.

1. Surveys and Questionnaires:

Surveys and questionnaires present standardized questions designed to assess various aspects of authenticity, such as transparency, consistency, and ethical behavior. Participants rate their leaders' behaviors on numerical scales, generating quantitative data that can be statistically analyzed to identify trends and differences among leaders.

2. 360-Degree Feedback:

360-degree feedback gathers input from peers, subordinates, superiors, and self-assessment to provide a comprehensive evaluation of a leader's authenticity. This multisource feedback offers a holistic view of the leader's impact on different stakeholders, highlighting areas of alignment and potential discrepancies between self-perception and others' perceptions.

3. Behavioral Observations:

Quantitative behavioral observations involve recording specific actions and behaviors exhibited by leaders. Researchers define a set of observable authenticity-related behaviors, such as admitting mistakes, listening actively, and showing empathy. These behaviors are quantified and tracked over time, enabling a data-driven assessment of authenticity.

COMBINING QUALITATIVE AND QUANTITATIVE APPROACHES

While qualitative and quantitative approaches offer distinct advantages, their synergy can provide a more complete understanding of a leader's authenticity. By integrating these methods, researchers can triangulate data, corroborate findings, and capture the intricate interplay between subjective experiences and measurable outcomes.

1. Triangulation:

Triangulation involves using multiple data sources or methods to validate and strengthen research findings. Qualitative insights gathered from interviews or observations can be compared with quantitative survey results. Consistencies or discrepancies between the two types of data provide a deeper understanding of authenticity.

2. Rich Contextualization:

Qualitative data enriches the context of quantitative findings. For instance, if a quantitative survey indicates that a leader is perceived as authentic by a majority of team members, qualitative interviews can elucidate the specific behaviors or communication styles that contribute to this perception.

3. Exploring Anomalies:

When discrepancies arise between qualitative and quantitative findings, further exploration is warranted. Anomalies may signal hidden complexities in the concept of authenticity or potential biases in the measurement instruments.

4. Mixed-Methods Research:

Conducting mixed-methods research involves collecting and analyzing both qualitative and quantitative data concurrently. This holistic approach offers a comprehensive understanding of authenticity, leveraging the strengths of both methodologies to provide a well-rounded assessment.

CONCLUDING THE
RESEARCH EXPLANATION

In the pursuit of measuring and understanding a leader's authenticity, a combination of qualitative and quantitative approaches proves to be a powerful methodology. Qualitative methods delve into the personal narratives, emotions, and behaviors that underpin authenticity, while quantitative methods provide structured data for statistical analysis and trend identification. The integration of these approaches through triangulation, contextualization, and mixed-methods research offers a holistic perspective that embraces both the complexity and measurability of authenticity in leadership. As organizations navigate the ever-evolving landscape of leadership, this combined approach serves as a compass, guiding the assessment and development of authentic leaders who inspire trust, foster engagement, and drive sustainable success.

AUTHENTIC LEADERSHIP
SELF-ASSESSMENT

Thank you for participating in this self-assessment focused on evaluating your authentic leadership qualities. Please respond to the following questions honestly, considering your behaviors, values, and interactions as a leader. Your insights will help you gain a better understanding of your authenticity and areas for growth.

Instructions: Rate each statement on a scale from 1 to 5, where:

- 1 = Strongly Disagree
- 2 = Disagree
- 3 = Neutral
- 4 = Agree
- 5 = Strongly Agree

Section 1: Consistency and Values

I consistently align my actions with my stated values and principles.

My decisions and behaviors reflect my authentic beliefs and convictions.

I am known for my unwavering commitment to ethical conduct.

1	2	3	4	5
Strongly Disagree	Disagree	Neutral	Agree	Strongly Agree

Section 2: Transparent Communication

I openly share information about organizational goals and challenges with my team.

I encourage open and honest discussions, even when opinions differ.

Team members feel comfortable approaching me with their concerns and ideas.

1	2	3	4	5
Strongly Disagree	Disagree	Neutral	Agree	Strongly Agree

Section 3: Self-Awareness and Humility

I am open about my own mistakes and take responsibility for them.

I actively seek feedback from others to improve my leadership.

I am comfortable acknowledging areas where I need to grow.

1	2	3	4	5
Strongly Disagree	Disagree	Neutral	Agree	Strongly Agree

Section 4: Empathy and Emotional Intelligence

I demonstrate understanding and empathy toward team members' feelings and concerns.

I genuinely listen to others without interrupting or rushing to conclusions.

I consider others' emotions when making decisions that affect them.

1	2	3	4	5
Strongly Disagree	Disagree	Neutral	Agree	Strongly Agree

Section 5: Values-Driven Decision-Making

I consistently make decisions that are aligned with our organization's core values.

I prioritize ethical considerations when making difficult choices.

I ensure that my decisions take into account the well-being of all stakeholders.

1	2	3	4	5
Strongly Disagree	Disagree	Neutral	Agree	Strongly Agree

Section 6: Building Genuine Relationships

I invest time in building meaningful and authentic relationships with team members.

I make an effort to know my team members on a personal level.

I show genuine concern for team members' growth and well-being.

1	2	3	4	5
Strongly Disagree	Disagree	Neutral	Agree	Strongly Agree

Section 7: Reflecting on Authenticity

I regularly reflect on my leadership behaviors and their alignment with my values.
I actively seek opportunities to enhance my authenticity as a leader.

1	2	3	4	5
Strongly Disagree	Disagree	Neutral	Agree	Strongly Agree

CONCLUDING THE SELF-ASSESSMENT

It may take time to work these issues into the goals of becoming an authentic leader. However, you can't use data you don't have. Once you see your results, look back through the book to see what tips there are for expanding on your strengths, lessening your weaknesses, and maybe even noticing blind spots. This will give you a place to start.

Points	8-24 Points	25-30 Points	30-35 Points
What They Mean	You are just beginning your journey. While there is a lot to learn, you have started simply by picking up this book.	You are coming along on this journey. Maybe this book even got you further!	You've got this journey down! Time to pass this book onto others.

Points	8-24 Points	25-30 Points	30-35 Points
What To Work On	Read through this book again and make sure you are doing all of the journal entries and exercises, and even take notes. Look at these seven areas and see where you need the most growth.	In your case, it is also important to read the rest of the book and reread parts you think you are struggling with. It can be especially helpful to start discussing this with others, as other people will have other insights, even if you are not ready to teach. Look at these seven areas and see where you need the most growth.	This book most likely made a significant impact on your thoughts, feelings, and actions. At this point, it is time to teach. Give someone else this book then take this test with them. You've got a head and a heart to lead! Look at these seven areas and see where you can instruct.

EXAMPLES

You might be pondering when these practices are applicable in your daily life. Here are instances along with designated journal spaces. In your reflections, consider identifying the steps taken and leadership styles employed. Evaluate whether you believe the leader handled the situation appropriately and contemplate if there are alternative approaches you could consider.

Example One:

Stephen runs his own business with over fifty employees, and they have a team huddle every week. Despite having some hybrid workers, Stephen wants everyone to come to the office for the huddle. Francine, a team member who is still new to the team, messages Stephen and says she did not know she needed to go in person, and she won't be able to make it there, as she is staying with her sick mother. Stephen allows her to call in to the first meeting with the promise that she will attend future meetings in person.

Evaluate whether you believe the leader handled the situation appropriately and contemplate if there are alternative approaches you could consider.

Example Two:

Brandy is in charge of a medium sized team at a fortune 500 company. One employee calls in every Monday, despite that always being their scheduled day. Brandy considers just firing them, but decides instead to discuss their situation. They explain that their child is a problem drinker, and they often have to spend Monday finding them after they disappear all weekend. The team member says it is exacerbated because they have so much work on the weekends. After the team member has explained the problem in detail, Brandy reminds them that the company health insurance includes drug and alcohol counseling and other services, and then she says that, while they cannot miss work, she can make sure they have no work to take home on weekends.

Evaluate whether you believe the leader handled the situation appropriately and contemplate if there are alternative approaches you could consider.

Example Three:

Daniel wonders if he is cut out for leadership, as he feels a bit unfettered. He decides to read this book and then find his purpose—he starts with looking into the vision statement of the company, then deep dives into his personal life to see how he feels about those qualities. When he finds the qualities he feels he most identifies with, he strengthens them, and when he finds the qualities he feels he needs the most work on, he builds from the ground up. He also asks his mentor if there are any qualities that he is lacking (that he may not know he is lacking).

Evaluate whether you believe the leader handled the situation appropriately and contemplate if there are alternative approaches you could consider.

Example Four:

Destinie learns that people higher up in her company are embezzling money. She knows this is hurting her employees, as they are receiving lower pay, getting less benefits, and are unaware of what is happening. She is not sure she can take this to the top but still decides to report them.

Evaluate whether you believe the leader handled the situation appropriately and contemplate if there are alternative approaches you could consider.

Example Five:

Luca wants to find a solution to a shipping problem in his small company. Despite only having a few employees, they are a tight-knit group, and he readily asks for their opinions. He thinks that he would get the most help from the woman who leads shipping, but Hosea, who is in charge of marketing, says he has an idea. Luca sets up a meeting with the man to get his opinion.

CULTIVATING AUTHENTIC LEADERSHIP: 10 COLLABORATIVE EXERCISES FOR BUILDING GENUINE CONNECTIONS WITH CO-WORKERS

In the pursuit of authentic leadership, fostering meaningful connections with colleagues is paramount. Here, we present ten dynamic exercises designed to not only enhance your authentic leadership skills but also to forge stronger bonds within your team. These activities are crafted to promote open communication, build trust, and encourage a shared commitment to authenticity. Engage in these exercises to unlock the full potential of authentic leadership in the collaborative context of the workplace. Each exercise is thoughtfully tailored to instill valuable insights and strengthen the interpersonal fabric of your professional relationships. Embrace these practices as opportunities for growth, reflection, and collective empowerment on your journey toward becoming an authentic leader in your team.

This section outlines ten exercises that can be practiced with co-workers to foster authentic leadership development.

1. Strengths Assessment:

Conduct a strengths assessment exercise to identify individual strengths within your team. Encourage each co-worker to share their unique abilities and talents. This exercise allows individuals to recognize their strengths and encourages others to acknowledge and appreciate those qualities. It sets a foundation for building authentic leadership by fostering self-awareness and appreciation among team members.

2. Active Listening Practice:

Organize a session focused on active listening skills. Pair co-workers and ask them to engage in a conversation where one person speaks while the other listens attentively. Afterward, encourage them to reflect on their listening experience, emphasizing the importance of active listening in effective leadership. This exercise cultivates empathy, understanding, and enhances communication skills.

3. Values Alignment:

Facilitate a discussion on personal values and their alignment with the organization's values. Encourage co-workers to explore their core principles and share how they resonate with the company's mission. This exercise promotes authenticity by encouraging individuals to align their personal values with their leadership style, fostering a sense of purpose and integrity.

4. Feedback Exchange:

Create a safe environment for honest feedback by organizing a feedback exchange session. Pair co-workers and ask them to provide constructive feedback to each other based on their observations. This exercise promotes trust, encourages open communication, and helps individuals improve their self-awareness and growth.

5. Decision-making Simulation:

Create a decision-making simulation exercise where co-workers are presented with real-life scenarios and asked to make decisions collectively. This exercise allows for collaboration, conflict resolution, and critical thinking. By navigating through these scenarios, co-workers can practice making decisions that align with their authentic leadership style.

6. Emotional Intelligence Training:

Arrange an emotional intelligence training session to help co-workers understand and manage their emotions effectively. Choose issues that cause heightened emotions in the workplace to discuss, such as having a review that goes poorly. Ask them how they respond. This exercise enhances self-awareness, empathy, and interpersonal skills, all of which are key aspects of authentic leadership.

7. Role-playing Scenarios:

Have coworkers design role-playing scenarios that require everyone to practice authentic leadership skills such as vulnerability, active listening, and empathy. This exercise encourages individuals to step into different leadership roles and gain insights into how their actions impact others, especially as they leave the roleplay. It also promotes adaptability and a deeper understanding of diverse perspectives.

8. Mentorship Program:

Implement a mentorship program where experienced leaders mentor junior co-workers. This exercise not only fosters professional growth but also creates an environment for authentic leadership development. Mentors can impart their wisdom, share experiences, and guide their mentees towards becoming authentic leaders.

9. Team-building Activities:

Engage in team-building activities that foster collaboration, trust, and open communication. Such activities could include problem-solving challenges, outdoor adventures, or team-building workshops. By participating in these exercises, co-workers learn to rely on each other's strengths, build relationships, and develop their own authentic leadership style within a team setting.

10. Mindfulness and Reflection:

Encourage co-workers to engage in mindfulness and reflection exercises to enhance self-awareness and promote personal growth. This could involve meditation sessions, journaling, or guided reflection exercises.

CONCLUSION

This book demonstrated the basics of how to be an authentic leader. Reading this book, however, is only the beginning of the journey to who you are becoming. There are several things that can help you get started. First, living out the steps, paired with answering the journal questions after them, will give you the beginning stages of making a change. After you have done this, meeting with other leaders and team members can further your learning. If you learn how to measure leadership, self-assess, and help your team to self-assess, you can lead a healthy team and see your strengths, weaknesses, and blind spots. These assessments include both qualitative and quantitative studies. While most likely not all your teammates are not in leadership, there are parts of this book that will be just as useful to them.

In addition to helping your teammates through sharing parts of this book, it will also help them when you become someone who exemplifies many of the leadership styles. Regarding the list of styles, one of the most important things you can do is answer the journal questions. Read each over carefully and, if it helps, rate them based on which ones you are strongest and weakest in. This will give you a chance to have an actual list of what to work on. This can also be done best with another person who will tell you about your blind spots.

The ten exercises to build authentic leadership skills should not be all done in one day. Rather, setting up a few team meetings with a decent amount of space in between can let your coworkers think through the exercises, and if they are coming up with them (like the role-playing scenario), it can be helpful to give them time. The examples can also involve them because while they focus on questions that come up for leaders, it can be worth seeing what ideas your employees have. After all, it involves them.

Overall, the best thing you can do is think long and hard about what you've learned from this book. Once you have some of these down, help others get them down, too. For now, focus on the growth mindset and lead with purpose.

Made in the USA
Middletown, DE
21 July 2024